TERRIAN JOURNALS'

HOW TO MAKE THE NATION:

an instruction book for nationalizing and colonizing human beings

By Donald Murray Anderson

MSB

Terrian Journals' How To Make The Nation

A Mythbreaker Book

2021 Edition

© Copyright 1983, 1987, 1989, 2009, 2010, 2013, 2014. 2021 by Donald Murray Anderson

ISBN 978-1-989593-16-5

For information address: mythbreaker@mail.com

<u>ACKNOWLEDGEMENT</u>

All of the nation-making techniques explained here are based on Europe's 460 years of colony-nation-making efforts and the ensuing work of nation-states everywhere.

However, here the techniques are made more obvious and explicit so that generations of nation-makers can be known for what they do to interhuman relations.

Note: Previous versions of <u>Terrian Journals' How to Make The Nation</u> (TJHTMTN) were published as an appendix to <u>A Sketch of Terrian History.</u>

The first appendix had 19 points.

The current edition of the separate volume version of TJHTMTN has grown to include 28 points and additional material providing a more complete picture of the nation.

The content of <u>Terrian Journals' How to Make The Nation</u> may be considered satirical or exaggeration, but much of what is written here is based on actual observation, as well as the content and presentation of information about "the nation" in books, news reports, documentaries, and conversations with nationalists in various parts of the world.

This book would be funny, if tens of millions of people had not died for "the nation" in international and monarchical war.

<u>FOREWORD</u>:

The nation is such a dominant preoccupation of humanity that a casual visitor to Earth might easily conclude that the nation is this planet's main lifeform, predating the existence of humans.

Thus nation-making is proving itself to be a very refined form of the art of illusion.

Nation-state makers show themselves to be very skillful at combining utter fantasy and sheer hallucination, the central foundations of the nation.

The nation is a toxic blend of mass hypnosis and mass hysteria with myriad injurious and fatal effects on human beings.

In the writing which follows, the reader can discover how nation-state makers make the nation, with little or no reference to facts or reality.

Donald Murray Anderson
(Cordoba, in the south of the Americas.*)

*Although originally inspired in the southern Americas, further additions to <u>How To Make The Nation</u> have come from subsequent experiences there, on the east and west coasts of Asafeur, and in Canada.

Introduction: NATIONED

Nationality is no more than conditioned behaviour, programming.

It is not natural or hereditary in any way. Nationality is entirely acquired, learned behaviour.

So improved interhuman relations demand that every human being know that there is a clear distinction between people and their programmed behaviour.

In real life, nationality is but an adjective, not a noun.

Nationalized people are like canned peaches, in that they are conditioned to believe that the can is their natural shell, not their peach skins.

People are confined to a sealed nationality tin lining, instead of being free to pursue their actual living human identity.

People are tinned, labelled, packaged, crated, and stored in the nation-state warehouses.

National names are just packing labels, no matter how elaborate, cumbersome, protective, reassuring, and concealing they may be in describing the real contents.

Squid is squid, despite the "calamari" label to make it palatable to dinners who are squeamish about squid.

Since people are neither tins nor calamari, the language expressing national labels imposed on humans needs to be modified in order to more clearly distinguish the packaging from the human content.

Calling humans the people of such and such nation-state is inadequate. Using the word "the" still makes them seem distinct from the rest of humanity.

It is thus better to use words like locals, non-locals, or people living in such and such a nation-state.

These nebulous terms contrast with the specific all-defining term "human" which applies to all people and expresses their common identity beyond borders.

"Human" can be scientifically described in great detail and with considerable accuracy. Health science research is a well-established field.

Human physiology and psychology are well described. They are natural. They are not defined by nation-state place of birth or residency.

Apart from inbreeding, due to excessive nation-state confinement and the consequent "racism" called

nationalism, genetics, genome, and hereditary characteristics are not artificial or national.

They are entirely natural to all humans.

If nation-state labels are to reflect what they are in
reality, nationality programming, a new naming
system needs to be applied to replace the current one.

This system can more accurately reflect, like a label on
canned peaches, the reality of human beings confined
to being the contents of a nation-state.

The canned peach reality means human beings are
programmed and conditioned into believing that they
are behaving in a certain manner due entirely to the
existence of the nation-state can.

They perceive themselves largely in terms that are
defined, prescribed, and dictated entirely by place of
birth and physical residency within a particular
nation-state.

To expose this obvious fallacious programming,
people living in a nation-state need to strip off the
false and misleading nation-state labels.

A first step in this process would be to discard the
"nationality" labels ending in suffixes such as -ian, -
an, -ese, -ish, etc.

Thus a person living within the boundaries of Canada would henceforth be called Canadad.

Other humans are thus Denmarked, Egypted, Thaid, Madagascard, USAed, Françaide, Mozambiqued, Iraqued, Tongad, Congoed, Chiled, Surinamed, Gaboned, Russiad, Finlanded or Suomied, Perud, Hondurased, Chuang Hwad, Hangood, Nihoned, Togod, Tibetted, Upper Voltad, Zimbabwed, Philippined, Belized, Czeched, Solvaked, Norwayed or Norged, Europed or ECed, New Guinead, etc.

...

Both citizenship and nationality are defined and redefined in the context of the nation-state name-calling.

Citizenship, unlike nationality, is a word that is honest about its artificiality.

Nationality is not.

Nationality is immersed in and imbued with specific, distinct characteristics which have no roots in the nation-state system, except in the sense of nation-states attempting to separate humanity by inventing and emphasizing a restricted list of human characteristics which the nation-state declares only exist in people living in nation-states and its people living abroad, called ex-pats or diaspora.

The restricted list of characteristics includes carefully and rigidly defined ones, defining culture, language, dialect, customs, physiology-psychology, and an array of habitual behaviours, including specific types of manners, characters, and personality traits.

Everything on this list underpins nation-states and the artificial official barriers they put between people.

Citizenship has no such pretensions.

According to legend, anyone in territories ruled by the military occupation forces of Rome's empire, anyone who was not a slave of Rome, could become a citizen of Rome.

Some nation-states today permit non-locals to convert to the citizenship of their locals.

Some trap newcomers by forcing them to renounce citizenship status in all other nation-states.

Other nation-states permit newcomers and locally-born people to hold citizenship in other nation-states.

People encounter difficulty when one nation-state insists on renunciation but another has no restrictions on the citizenships of locals.

The sole objective of making the nation is thus to manipulate people's perceptions of themselves and their personal identities so that they will perceive themselves as the entirely distinct creation, dependants, devotees, and faithful servants of the nation.

In truth, nationality and citizenship are entirely artificial, total fiction and illusions created to confuse, inhibit, and restrict human advancement by confining us all to cans called nations, and to insist that we cannot live together in peace as one form of life on our common home place planet.

Nationism

The nation is the self-sustaining source and result of nationalism and its equally gruesomely deformed cohorts – chauvinism, xenophobia, and racism.

The nation religiously institutionalizes all of the above in "immigration" and "citizenship" ministries.

The nation enforces all of the above with border guards.

Introduction to more points

This edition of <u>Terrian Journals' How To Make The Nation</u> fills a gap with the addition of three new points: National Taxation, National Emergency, and National Currency.

These points are significant omissions from all previous editions.

*National Taxation recognizes that no matter how zealous, committed, harsh, and/or sadistic the nation-state employees may be, they remain at heart mere mercenaries, at least in the sense of needing the nation as a means to supply themselves with basic life-support and much more.

Thus, special nation-state employees need to cajole, trick, persuade, or force nation-state captives to support the nation-state financially.

If the captives don't pay the nation-state bills, the captives serve no purpose and so should be eliminated.

*National Emergency unveils an essential internal tool in the arsenal of nation-building when the nation is at risk of collapsing due to growing or potentially growing awareness among the human residents of the irrelevance and redundancy of the nation and its anti-human bases.

Externally linked and internally generated sudden and alarming grave crises need to be belatedly recognized, highlighted, and accentuated to rally "the people" around the nation, if out of nothing more than fear and other feelings of incertitude and personal insecurity.

The nation resorts to declaring a national emergency when there are indications that there is insufficient gullibility among the people to enable the nation to generate and maintain the amount of hostility required to set off, sustain, and prolong the duration of a perpetual all-out war without armed conflict against the "outside world".

*National currency places a monetary value on the nation and the people within it.

The national currency is an ever-changing alphabetic, numeric, and pictorial representation of the artificial economic foundation underlying and undermining the nation and its credibility in the eyes of the people.

Contents

16.Packaging national history, historic sites, monuments, & parks

17.Preaching national ideology and religion

18.Writing the national constitution and laws

19.Selecting politicians and bureaucrats

20.Engraving National Currency in the people's minds

21.Calculating national economy

22.Taxation

23.Declaring the national emergency

24.Making war, treaties, trade, immigration, and citizenship

25.Constructing the national wall and free trade agreement with tariffs

26.Planning national travel

27.Building the empire

28.Activating the national armed forces and police

Forewarning

No matter where you are born or where you will live, someone, at one time or another, is bound to try to invent a nation-state around you.

Unfortunately, it is then you who is left in a bind, bound by the nation-state.

1. NAMING THE NATION:

The most concrete and substantive part of the nation is its name. The nation cannot exist before it has a name.

The purpose of the nation's name is to tell people where they are.

Human beings have a long history of being deprived of knowing that they are in the nation.

The nation's name can be any word or combination of words. It should also be easy to pronounce and have almost no significance whatsoever for anyone.

2. DRAWING BOUNDARIES AND IDENTIFYING FOREIGNERS:

Once the nation has a name, the national boundaries can be drawn.

The boundaries cannot be drawn before the nation has a name because signs at the borders would have to be left blank.

National boundaries are necessary to show where the nation is located.

Without boundaries, the nation could be anywhere.

Boundaries are also prerequisite to handing out national identification to some people but not others.

After the boundaries are drawn, every person who happens to be living within them at the time can be given a piece of identi-fication.

The identification is the only way that they will be able to tell the difference between themselves and the foreigners.

Without boundaries and identification, anyone could be either a member of the nation, (a national), or a foreigner.

A national can only be a person who hap-pens to reside on the nation's territory when the national boundaries are drawn.

A foreigner can only be a person who hap-pens to reside outside of the nation's terri-tory when the national boundaries are drawn.

Drawing national boundaries is thus the only means of differentiating between a national and foreigner.

Without national boundaries, a foreigner cannot be identified because s/he is indistinguishable from a national.

Nationals and foreigners are no different than other naturally mobile animals and birds or dust and plant seeds blowing in the wind across the national boundaries.

Thus, without national boundaries and identification, border guards would be unable to challenge anyone crossing the nation's boundaries.

Every human being would be free to go anywhere in the world at will and to remain there for as long as s/he needs to or desires, without any restrictions.

What nation-fearing person would want to live in that kind of world?

We would all be like other animals and birds, migrating naturally according to the seasons and related food supplies.

It would revive a world of planet-without-unnatural-borders enabling a resurgence of human migration.

What a nightmare world that would be, for the nation.

The nation requires boundaries because the nation is inherently diametrically opposed to that world of human freedom-of-movement rights.

The nation requires boundaries because it is rooted in the domains of monarchies.

The nation is still run by the court*, i.e. a permanent bureaucracy evading and tolerating the attempted "political interference" of passing politicians.

(* Ironically, in nations including Canada, the nation's court swears allegiance to the monarchy, not to the nation.)

In short, the nation requires national boundaries because if it did not have them the populace would not know where they lived; they could not be confined and required to possess national identification; and that would undermine the whole concept of nation and risk the rebirth of natural instincts which could bring about a planetary human union fostering world peace.

National boundaries thus perform a public service to protect the nation from humanity.

Although completely arbitrary and meaningless in the natural world order, everyone must consider the national boundaries absolute and divine to ensure the survival of the nation.

The survival of the nation requires that everyone strictly observe and submit to the national boundaries.

This submission is helped if the national boundaries enclose only one continuous area of land.

No other restriction applies to boundary drawing.

The boundaries can be straight lines or wiggly ones with loops and odd shaped appendages.

Above all: No one must be permitted to realize that the national boundaries are fraudulent and meaningless in the real world beyond the illusion and delusions of the nation.

Thinking of this type is treasonous and heretical and can only bring eternal damnation.

3. EXPLAINING NATIONAL WEATHER AND CLIMATE

Once the national boundaries are set, the national meteorological agency can be created to publish descriptions of the distinctive and particular characteristics of the national climate.

The national climate exists nowhere else and there are no similar climates anywhere.

The national climate is the ideal climate, the best of all climates.

Thus, the people living within the national boundaries will want to remain forever within the perfect climate comfort zone provided by the nation.

Climate change would be treasonous.

The national meteorological agency will also issue national weather forecasts, illustrated with maps showing only the nation.

The maps show that all the good weather develops inside the national boundaries.

On the other hand, unpleasant weather and terrible storms are intrusions from outside the nation.

Bad weather experiences always start entirely and exclusively in places outside the national boundaries.

4. ESTABLISHING NATIONAL COMMUNICATIONS AND TRANSPORTATION:

The national system of communications and transportation are established by cutting the nation off from the everywhere else on Earth.

The people see everywhere beyond the national boundaries as far away, difficult to reach, expensive, and unpleasant.

Otherwise, the long term historical natural global human migration and unregulated contact with foreigners might reemerge.

The best national communications and transportation links are as far away as possible from the national boundaries.

Official boundary-crossing points are in areas most likely to experience frequent avalanches, severe year-round flooding, earthquakes, extreme climatic conditions, or be reputedly full of thieves, dangerous wild animals, or lost tribes of head hunters.

Roads and railways leading out of the nation are poorly designed and constructed with poor materials.

Air traffic control at the borders is unclear due to static and interference.

All broadcasts from foreign sources are jammed. All foreign internet broadcasts should be "unavailable in your country".

National news and information provides very minimal and distorted reports about foreign areas.

These reports deal exclusively with problems, disasters, and dangers.

5. DESCRIBING NATIONAL IDENTITY AND PRIDE:

National identity and pride are established by (i) issuing souvenirs of the nation for the people who live there, and (ii) by printing lists describing what constitutes the national identity and explaining why to have national pride.

When souvenirs and lists are well and widely distributed, the people should actually begin to believe that they have national identity and pride.

Thus the people will not be embarrassed or feel foolish when asked about their identity and pride.

On the contrary, those who ask such questions can be dismissed as ignorant or foreigners.

It will be apparent that no one who considers his/herself a member of the nation would ever need to ask questions.

6. ORGANIZING THE NATIONAL WAY OF LIFE:

The national way of life is organized by ensuring that the people are captives of a virtually monotonous, routine daily experience.

Life is replaced by national standards and correct, proper, but unwritten national codes of conduct.

National formats and systems minimize variations.

The nationals are persuaded to support the national way of life on the grounds that the foreigners want to destroy it.

7. DEFINING THE NATIONAL FOOD AND DIET

Defining the national food and diet can be the easiest aspect of nation building.

It requires only that the nation-state complete an inventory of everything edible within the national boundaries and then publish it as a comprehensive list.

Append to the list purely fictional, glowing "scientific" reports about the unique appearance, flavour, taste, and nutritional value of the national food.

Reports will unequivocally state that this food is only found inside the national boundaries.

Naturally, "science" of this kind also reaches the irrefutable conclusion that it is impossible to find the national food anywhere outside the nation.

It is impossible to reproduce or to imitate those special characteristics and high qualities of the national food anywhere outside the nation.

Only the national soil, water, and air can support them.

Any foreign food which might appear to be exactly the same is, in reality, either mediocre or an authentic sample of national food which has been clandestinely and illegally smuggled out of the nation and then falsely labelled.

To protect the nation from outrageously false declarations that the national food actually originates elsewhere, recently or long ago, the nation-state will discredit and erase all similarly tainted and ludicrous historic records and memory.

There can be no tolerance for misinformation indicating that some long-established national staple, such as potatoes or tomatoes, was actually introduced from some foreign place lacking the very special soil and climate of the nation.

If anyone questions or criticizes the quality or taste of the national food, rumours can be spread about foreign spies contaminating the national food supply, or foreign-based exporters sending the highest quality national food abroad, depriving the nationals of the best of the national food.

Rumours of this sort will help the nation by reinforcing the people's hostility toward the foreigners, especially those who are eating the best food of the nation.

Rumours of this sort will also encourage a great outcry against exporting any national food to the outside world.

Of course the nation may also export some good quality national food abroad, but only out of pity for the foreigners because they are doomed to living in places which can never grow the national food.

However, as a general rule, foreigners should only be able to export spoiled, substandard, and otherwise inedible national food to places beyond the national boundaries.

If foreigners could taste the best of the national food, they would thereafter find their foreign food tasteless and impalatable.

They would be more likely to attempt to invade the nation just to eat the national food.

Defining the national food and diet also means writing and demonstrating the nation's recipe book.

There can only be two conclusions: 1) The national cuisine is exquisite. And, 2) The national chefs are the most competent and best chefs in the world.

The nation is the homeland of absolute and ultimate food preparation genius. Foreigners may come to study the process, but none will truly understand or master it.

The people of the nation will pity the foreigners who are on non-national diets, i.e. consuming unappetizing and bad tasting meals which have no nutritional value whatsoever, prepared by substandard cooks using flawed and poorly copied recipes.

8. DECLARING THE OFFICIAL NATIONAL LANGUAGE AND CULTURE:

If the national boundaries enclose a very small area of land and few people, the work of declaring the official national language and culture is simplified considerably.

The people need never be informed of the declaration.

The official national language, for any size population, is preferably a language not used by any of the people.

That enables everyone to unite in opposition to the official language. National unity is born.

Larger populations pose a more complicated problem only because it may be necessary to declare several official languages to stimulate everyone into united opposition.

The official national culture is much simpler to declare than the language.

The declaration is vague and refers to the actual cultures of the people as quaint and colourful regional variations.

Problems arise when the official language or culture is identical to that of the foreigners.

The national academy of language and culture must publish dictionaries and other books reporting the results of "earned studies" which conclude that the nation has unique and distinct national word usage, pronunciation, meaning, and spelling, as well as unusual customs and dress.

9. IDENTIFYING TYPICAL NATIONAL RACIAL CHARACTERISTICS:

The typical national racial characteristics require more imagination than the national language and culture.

The nation must be seen as a place filled with people who nature has endowed with very special attributes which, of course, are superior to those of the foreigners.

The people of the nation have an intangible similarity to each other, which attracts friends and frightens enemies.

A foreigner is so markedly and strikingly different that no one need ever discuss the national racial characteristics.

The people should be told to consider them obvious. Everyone knows.

10. DESIGNING THE NATIONAL FLAG AND SYMBOLS:

The national flag and symbols are peculiar looking signboards designed to make the nation appear to be a constant presence in the people's lives.

This helps conceal the fact that the nation is completely irrelevant to natural human experiences.

Everywhere the nation must make its peculiar and irrelevant presence known.

The flag and symbols are comprised of things such as geometric shapes, stripes, crosses, animals, feathers, plants, stars, bands of colour, or whatever seems to be eye-catching, convenient, and easy to duplicate.

If anyone should ask for an explanation of the flag or symbols, a colourful story can be made up.

If plants or animals are used in the flag or symbols, preference should be given to those which can actually live in the nation.

If none are already there, they can be said to be extinct.

Or, non-native plants or animals may be brought into the nation before the flag and symbols are announced to the people.

In the event that the people witness the planting or distribution of national plants and animals, it can be said that the nation operates farms to breed and conserve these national resources.

11. COMPOSING THE NATIONAL ANTHEM AND RELATED OFFICIAL MUSIC:

The official national music is composed to arouse the emotions of the people toward loving something with which they can never share the feelings of a human relationship – the nation.

Of all blind love, the nation demands the blindest.

At the sound of a tune, with vaguely poetic words attached, the people are expected to be awed.

They should cry, smile, be happy, be serious, and be solemn, all at once. They should stand quietly, preferably rigidly.

The national music is performed ceremoniously before the people, at selectively chosen moments called customary and appropriate occasions.

These moments should be frequent enough to prevent the people from forgetting the music.

To reinforce memory, such tunes are often played before sporting events, followed by the loud cheering of crowds relieved that the strange music is finished and the games can finally begin.

12. COMPOSING NATIONAL MARCHES AND ADOPTING FOLKLORIC MUSIC:

National marches are drum music to make the people all move in the same direction, without first considering if it is where they actually want to go.

They can only go where the nation points when the band starts playing.

National folkloric music is something to listen to during rest periods between marches.

Nations must adopt the existing music of the people because the nation has no basis in folklore.

If the people listen to folkloric music too often, the nation can drown it out with marches.

13. DESIGNATING NATIONAL HOLIDAYS:

The main value of the national holiday is that it tends to make the people use the word national all day in conjunction with pleasant personal experiences.

No one needs to know that there is any reason for the holiday beyond the fact that the nation exists.

Without the nation there can be no holidays, the people should conclude.

14. CREATING NATIONAL HEROES, LEGENDS, AND MYTHS:

National heroes, legends, and myths provide great opportunities for exciting fiction writing.

The nation is given a colourful appearance.

The people gain stories about persons and events which everyone realizes are false but which everyone believes.

At the same time, the foreigners are left completely mislead and confused.

Most legends and myths are related to the biographies of national heroes.

These people do something extraordinary which the nation later calls efforts for the nation.

Thus biographies can be filled with flattering portraits, thrilling accounts, and quotations lauding the nation.

Lost and forgotten speeches, diaries, and memoirs can be written now and again and then publicly "discovered" to keep the people interested.

If any foreigners try to poach a national hero and claim her or him as their own, it is only because foreigners are all jealous liars.

15. PROMOTING NATIONAL SPORTS AND NATIONAL GAMES:

Promoting national sports and games is an extension and logical conclusion of creating national heroes, legends, and myths.

The nation itself is widely understood to be the source of all physical energy and athletic skills.

The people of the nation are born with a natural prowess for the national sports and the national games.

Every child born in the nation will almost immediately demonstrate a natural ability and knack for the national sport.

The people of the nation will proudly point at the national children kicking a ball for the first time and declare them so strong and skilled that they are absolute, living proof that people in the nation are naturally endowed to play the national kick ball sport.

The people of the nation are also born to instinctively cheer, shout, laugh, jump, pound walls, stamp feet, weep, cry out in orgasmic delight, and otherwise gesticulate to show their inborn, heightened emotions at the very sight of people playing the national sports, even during obvious lulls in action, intermissions, and post-game hours.

The more national mass hysteria accompanying the national sports, the more the people demonstrate their love and loyalty to the nation.

The people are the national sports fans, bursting with joy in their zealous devotion to the nation creating sports and games.

Supporting the national sports and games is an outpouring of joy and pride in the nation.

The national sports and games players are super nationals, idols to worship and emulate in their demonstration of the skills with which the nation endows them.

The national sports and games players are invincible role models for all to follow.

They participate in sports and games against the foreigners only to further expose the foreigners' inferiority and to rally the people in unquestioning support for the nation.

The national sports and games players always emerge victorious.

The results of sports and games against foreigners only appear otherwise if the fanatical foreigners are unfairly permitted to exhibit their normal poor character by cheating, corruption, violence, and causing bad weather to attack playing fields.

16. PACKAGING NATIONAL HISTORY, HISTORIC SITES, MONUMENTS, & PARKS:

National history, historic sites, monuments, and parks are created to make the national past and present appear to coincide.

The nation must seem to be a natural conclusion of the past.

The history of the nation need only be a list of names and dates with adjectives which can be changed whenever the nation requires a revision of an historical interpretation.

Revision, reinterpretation, and large-scale rewriting of the national history go unquestioned due to the invention of new sources of historical information and the eventual deaths of people who witnessed real past events.

The historic sites and monuments are created by erecting signs on pieces of land with no financial value.

Signs present brief, vague descriptions of what makes the site historic.

Description signs should be made of materials which appear substantial but which quickly fade, deteriorate, and disintegrate.

This indicates the permanence of the nation and allows for both substantial revisions as needed and relocation of the national historic site if land prices increase.

Another type of historic site is the national park – a rural area where the nation claims to be responsible for the continued existence of nature.

There, nature is said to be preserved only because the nation protects it.

As the ultimate guardian of nature, the nation will increase the number and size of national parks until geological exploration, as well as drilling and mining are required to fuel the nation.

Without the nation, there could be no alpine meadows, lakes, rivers, streams, forests, or animals in their natural state.

Human beings in their natural state, without the nation, neglect to build park gates, picnic tables, flush toilets, hot showers, paved parking, and forest ranger stations.

These humans also do not pause to label nature trails with kilometre and direction signs.

They do not give trees and flowers the name tags that these plants need.

17. PREACHING NATIONAL IDEOLOGY AND RELIGION:

National ideology and religion are used to justify anything and everything the nation does and can do.

The nation can act in contradictory and absolutely opposite ways, always supported by the national ideology and religion.

Both cosmic and terrestrial sources are thus allies of the nation.

These absolute sources of national morality seem clear, precise, and exacting, but are never to be considered before any plan or act of the nation.

Only the people should become devout followers of the national ideology and religion so that the nation can be free to take whatever action is necessary.

When the people are followers, the nation can lead them anywhere.

The people know that the nation itself is the one and only true ideology and religion.

The nation is the one and only true deity, supreme being.

18. WRITING THE NATIONAL CONSTITUTION, AND LAWS:

The national constitution and laws can be used as a substitute for ideology and religion. They are interchangeable.

Since very few of the people will ever read the national constitution and laws, they need not be written.

Why divert the nation from important, practical matters?

It is sufficient to say that the documents exist.

If necessary, sentences can be written later and called quotations.

If actually written, the constitution should be long and uninteresting to read.

The laws should be so poorly written and so confusing as to be incomprehensible to anyone who thinks clearly and rationally.

The nation can thus declare the documents complicated and wise, requiring expert study and interpretation.

Another possibility is to have only laws and no constitution.

The result can be called an unwritten constitution.

It never requires amendment and is completely safe from scrutiny and revision by the people.

Whatever option is chosen, written or unwritten, it is left to lawyers and judges to interpret words which do or do not exist.

19. SELECTING POLITICIANS AND BUREAUCRATS:

The national politicians and bureaucrats are responsible for making decisions that the people themselves would make if the nation did not exist.

Without the nation, there is thus no purpose or function for politicians or bureaucrats.

The nation requires these servants to perpetuate its existence because the nation is an unnatural entity.

The natural, long-term experience, judgement, logic, decisions, and participation of the people in their own lives does not require the planning or formation of the nation.

The artificial basis of the nation is that:

> i) the people's experience can be ignored because no one knows who the people of the nation are until after the boundaries are drawn; and,

> ii) every aspect of the nation has to be ready at that moment so that the nation can function smoothly, without the involvement or interference of the people.

> Their role is to work and serve.

> The nation provides for their comfort and convenience, instead of letting the people exercise their minds by thinking and decision-making.

To serve the nation to its unnatural end, politicians and bureaucrats require certain special qualities.

They are selected on the basis of gullibility, pomposity, and physical appearance.

No other people could be seriously interested in political or bureaucratic positions.

The work of politicians and bureaucrats is to attract and distract the people.

Elections and meetings are held to give the people a sense of participation without compromising or jeopardizing the nation by actual participation.

The people become too accustomed to comfort and convenience to participate in their own lives.

Politicians and bureaucrats also divert criticism from the nation.

Problems are seen as a result of them instead of the existence of the nation.

Politicians make speeches praising the nation and ridiculing bureaucrats and other politicians.

At the same time, bureaucrats try to make politicians look foolish, and invent procedures and regulations which waste as much of the people's time and finances as possible.

Together politicians and bureaucrats make the people act increasingly like dependants of the nation by discouraging them from taking care of their own needs.

Everything becomes nationally planned and constructed.

The people begin looking to the nation, not themselves, as the source of sustenance of human life.

They value national currency more than themselves.

20. ENGRAVING NATIONAL CURRENCY IN THE PEOPLE'S MINDS

The nation uses national currency to evaluate the people and to let them know exactly what they are worth.

The national elite are worth more and the rest of the people are worthless.

The nation's prime goal and feature of inequality is thus ensured.

In the nation, most of the people must possess the least wealth so that they will always be dependants of the nation.

They must always know that the nation is their master and that they cannot live without it.

This is probably the origin of the tears the people shed when they hear the national anthem.

Dependent people automatically lack the means of doing much beyond the confines of the national way of life and are much less likely to stray beyond the national boundaries.

The people are "poor but happy" to be kept alive by the nation. Their obedience is secured.

National currency is also a sure means by which the nation can make sure that the people do not forget the name of the nation or those of the deceased national heroes and politicians.

National currency is engraved and/or printed on tokens and paper displaying the name of the nation and a rough likeness of a dead hero or politician.

In some nations and during some eras, the reigning titular but powerless monarch also appears on the national currency.

If the national economy falters, the figurehead monarch can be blamed.

The people will carry a collection of national currency tokens and paper everywhere they go and look at it every time they need food, clothing, transportation, or services.

The national currency is a constant reminder of the essential existence of the nation.

Thus for the foreseeable future, even in an age of cheques, credit cards, and payment by computer banking, the least moneyed non-elite must continue to feel that they must cling to the token and paper currency for a long time.

The nation does not rush to take all the tokens and paper from the least moneyed non-elite because it's wide usage devalues the people and reduces their mobility.

Discount transportation prices make the point.

They are only available on computer websites, ensuring that they are most easily accessible to the more moneyed people who don't need any discounts because they can afford to pay full price.

If most of the people became like the elite ticket buyers, i.e. did not prize and use the national currency in the form of tokens and paper, or other materials bearing the nation's name, that would have dire economic consequences that would be a great threat to the nation.

The people would lose their daily reminders of the nation's existence.

The people could become mobile and their self-esteem and self-expectations could rise.

If electronic currency were to completely replace the national currency, the nation would probably have to shut down the national mint and bank too.

To fully understand the significance of national currency for the nation, it is important to know that the national currency is a precious commodity for the nation with a fluctuating history.

National currency tokens begin as national coins made of a precious metal such as gold and silver.

When gold and silver becomes too valuable to leave in the hands of the people, the metals of the national currency are changed to nickle, bronze, copper, tin, and/or aluminium coins.

The gold and silver coins can thus become the centre of a planned economic meltdown, putting gold and silver into the national coffers.

Coins become known for their lack of worth, as well as their bulk, weight, and resulting bulges in people's pockets and change purses.

Panhandlers try to lessen this burden by asking for "spare change". Automated toll gates on national roads demand payment in change for many years.

The nation eliminates some national coins by creating paper national money called bank notes or bills that are given out in exchange for the coins.

The nation can then melt down any non-circulating coins that still contain valuable metals.

The economic meltdown continues.

This papering over of the economy accomplished, the nation will begin to change some smaller bills into coins made of non-precious metals.

National conversion from coins to paper and then back to coins again is always described as a money-saving measure for the convenience of the people.

Then the nation eliminates smaller coins, especially ones made of copper when that metal becomes more valuable than the coin using it.

Another meltdown will ensue.

The people will buy back the copper in coins that they exchange for paper money, in the form of pipes for plumbing, electric wiring, etc.

In the end, the resulting national currency is made of cheap metals and paper.

The elimination of smaller denomination national coins is also a means of both fuelling and concealing inflation.

By eliminating the 1 unit coin, for example, prices can be raised so that they can be "rounded off" to the nearest higher unit coin.

Since there are no longer any 1 unit coins, the seller can literally keep the change difference.

After all the back and forth switches and eliminations in the national currency become norms for the people, another change can be made.

All surviving paper national currency can be eliminated without reverting to an all coin national currency or an electronic one.

Paper can be replaced with plastic.

This will help the poor old big oil companies facing lower mega-profits due to the disappearance of internal combustion engines, petroleum-fuelled electric power grids, oil furnaces, synthetic fibre clothing, plastic bottles, and supermarket plastic bags.

The nation will explain, with a straight face, that plastic currency lasts five times longer than paper currency. So it is more economical to replace paper with plastic.

The nation will only whisper that the plastic currency is five times more expensive to create than paper currency.

When the nation has plastic currency it is also much easier to bring about another economic melt-down.

Just leave the national currency near something very hot.

...

No matter how many twists and turns the national currency takes, including new designs or raised imprints; colour and face changes; symbols that set off security alarms; tiny dots removable with a pin; magnetic strips that peal off accidentally; shiny holographs; and taking three zeros off the bills; the national currency must instill absolute confidence in the nation and ensure advantageous rates of exchange.

An advantageous exchange rate means that the national currency is kept low and in decline abroad while causing inflation within the nation.

This helps sellers avoid competing with foreigners and enables the people to understand that national products are so superior that they must have the highest prices that the market will bear.

Maintaining low and declining exchange rates abroad is particularly important for maximizing the benefits of trade agreements with the foreigners.

Everything that the foreigners want to sell becomes too expensive for most of the people in the nation.

Everything that the nation sells abroad becomes a bargain.

Within the nation, the surge in sales to the foreigners is explained by saying that the foreigners' products are of such poor quality that foreigners are desperate to buy the nation's superior products.

...

Multinational currencies and the adoption of other nations' currencies must be avoided at all cost.

The people in the nation might start to believe they are the same as the foreigners or that they are members of a larger human community.

That would bring ruin to the nation.

21. CALCULATING THE NATIONAL ECONOMY:

By its very nature, the national economy is the most nebulous, poorly-thought-out, vague, and carelessly planned aspect of the nation.

Calculating the national economy requires national bookkeepers and statisticians who are dedicated to obscuring and falsifying data so that they reflect the nation's version of finance rather than the actual experiences of daily reality.

Bookkeeping is about balancing the national necessities against insufficient funds.

There are ample national financial resources, forthcoming or borrowed, to pay for all the national economic necessities.

The national economic necessities include tax cuts accompanied by substantial spending on, and/or generous subsidizing of, mammoth commercial projects, as well as payments to defend the nation against the foreigners.

Foreigners can never be trusted. They are always bellicose. They want to overrun and rule the world.

Such important responsibilities are best left exclusively to the nation.

At the same time, of course, the nation wisely controls and limits superfluous, luxury spending, such as food, shelter, human rights, and maintaining the planetary life support system.

It would be nice to have them all, but they are obviously too expensive and thus impractical.

Besides, after all, the planetary life support system is primarily used for keeping the foreigners alive, not the national people.

The national economy is for the benefit of the national people, not the foreigners.

Calculating the national economy starts with the underlying fact that the nation is the source and guarantor of all material prosperity for the national people.

They are unquestionably better off, in all respects, than the foreigners. Those poor devils.

The national economy encompasses taxation, spending, surpluses, deficits, debts, inflation, and employment.

Under the nation's care, taxation is low, spending is high, deficits are nil, debts are payable, inflation is negligible (i.e. completely neglected, hidden, and understated), and the national people are fully, totally employed (i.e. the nation uses them).

Problems with any of these basic matters are always totally attributable to the world outside the nation, i.e. the foreigners.

22. NATIONAL TAXATION:

Taxation is the nation's most powerful non-violent means of impoverishing, coercing, and incarcerating people living inside or outside the national boundaries.

Taxation's most appropriate definition thus comes from its usage in at least Canadian French, wherein taxation is the equivalent of the English word "bullying".

In the official national dogma and jargon, budgets, deficits, debts, and "the" economy are the rationale for national taxation.

They are for the common good, i.e. the common good of the nation itself.

It's quite uncommon for taxation to be a good in itself.

Taxation is not intended to produce an equitable, fair, or just redistribution of wealth.

Taxation is a funnel, not a sprinkler system.

If ever the reckless and mindless extreme concepts of the redistribution of wealth, i.e. taking money away from the nation, were to enter the dormant brain of a rogue agent of national taxation, such an agent would be quickly snuffed out because it risks catalyzing a mass awakening in the distracted minds of the human populace.

Human beings could do the unthinkable, i.e. attempt to overthrow the rule of the nation.

Human rule is anathema to the nation's stability and a threat to the national world order.

If any nation were to embark upon the self-destructive and suicidal path of equity, fairness, and justice for humanity, it would likely cause mass human migration to what would then become the anti-nation, a base of operations to liberate humanity from the nation everywhere and to eliminate the nation altogether.

The nation cannot allow humanity to regain control over its home planet.

Thus, the importance of maintaining a national system of taxation based on inequity, unfairness, and injustice cannot be exaggerated.

The entire history of taxation is one of imposing and enforcing such a system to end and prevent the return of a united and mobile human community.

The origins of taxation pre-date the nation.

In the insignificant and fictional past, i.e. before the nation, monarchical dictatorships rule the world. They are called monarchy for short.

Monarchy is a transitional pre-nation regime setting the foundations for absolute, divine-right nation-state rule.

Monarchy begins the work of forcibly and violently dividing the human community and eliminating free human movement.

Humans are rendered subjected, subjugated, and subservient.

The monarchy's abbreviation of these states of captivity is "subjects".

In fact human beings under monarchy might just as accurately be described as "objects", since they take the brunt of the tyrannically brutal and absolutist rule of monarchical dictators.

In this manner, subjects are converted into "loyal" subjects by effectively suspending human rights.

Anyone who is disobedient or rebellious, i.e. a person who hesitates or refuses to pay for the court's spending, is literally suspended in mid-air.

The subject is suspended "live", in a public place, where s/he is disentrailed by the monarch's taxation thugs, leaving her/his inner corporeal organs to hang out and become an inviting feast for passing hungry birds as well as the rats climbing along the means of suspension.

In those easier times for the very few, when no rationales or concealment were required for the elites' cruellest and greediest behaviours, monarchical dictators and their courts need only "make an example of someone" to elicit unconditional and complete devotion and obedience to paying for the extravagances and excesses of the elite court at the cost of mass suffering, starvation, and death, including "just" wars.

"Just" simply means only, since the only casualties of war are the "subjects", i.e. objects of the monarchy.

Any casualties or, "god forbid" deaths suffered by the monarch and/or court would be mainly caused by the objects' failure to get themselves killed, leaving the monarch and court elite in the line of fire.

Other monarch and/or court "casualties of war" would be deliberate assassinations within the monarchical dictatorship, or official suicides motivated by boredom with the shallow and empty existence of the elites' monotonous affluence and privilege.

The nation-state's failure to preserve the most violent force, i.e. pomp and ceremony, of taxation's time-dishonoured traditions under monarchy, is no doubt a source of sad regret in the greedy eyes of the nation's tax collectors.

In the nation-state, all the extravagance, torture, and bloodshed of monarchy need to be hidden away or eliminated, except for war.

War is retained due to its great value in protecting the nation safe from the threat of unity and mobility among the over-whelming majority of humanity.

War helps to prevent such an anti-nation outcome by culling the masses and regularly throwing them into grief and disarray.

Dead people cannot unite or move.

Physically and psychologically wounded people are too frightened and traumatized to do so. They only desire a "normal life".

The nation encourages and thrives on the "normal life".

For the nation, "normal life" means a disunited and immobile human populace.

It is no coincidence that taxation can also be defined as a war on humanity by peaceful, coercive means.

No matter how much propaganda the nation produces with taxation monies, to falsely label itself "democratic" and to declare itself a "free" haven from the threat of renewed human unity and mobility, taxation is no more than one of the last vestiges and legacies of monarchical dictatorship.

Taxation enforcers, now made over with the more innocuous title of "revenue agents", enjoy near monarchical privilege and legal immunity, while maintaining the monarchical dictatorship's traditional moral indifference and unchallengeable and thus unchecked ineptitude.

Like "order fillers" in the domain of marketing and sales, revenue agents are form fillers and adding machines.

It is vital that the revenue agents have a sense of being completely lost and that they exhibit intense intolerance if they are deprived of a form having all the blanks filled in.

If something is not recorded in the form, i.e. not "on file", it does not exist and need never be considered by the revenue agent.

The revenue agent form fillers must always find the actual facts of real life in their natural state both incomprehensible and disturbing.

The revenue agents' job qualifications must not include empathic hearts and thoughtful brains, just adoration of the nation and blind devotion to it.

The coffers of monarchy, now the nation's treasury, must be in a constant state of replenishing to ensure a steady flow of spending as if there were no tomorrow.

The human costs are of no consequence, mere collateral damage without any importance whatsoever.

The essential job requirement of the revenue agent is dedication to employing craftiness, treachery, and sleaziness, in the tradition of monarchical dictatorship.

The revenue agent's first non-principle and axiom is to collect the maximum from the poorest and the weakest and to render the entire populace poor and weak, except the court, now renamed the nation.

In this sense, taxation is like a resource town's "company store" and the precarious survival of humanity is a resource that must be striped away and depleted.

The revenue agent's sole purpose and objective is to protect the agent and the agent's master, the nation.

No life matters.

So long as the nation is overwhelmingly strong and humanity is underwhelmingly weak, all is well in the realm.

All resistance, questioning, complaints, and challenges originating with humanity must be crushed with ruthless force in the spirit of monarchical dictatorship.

Only the physical violence of monarchy is avoided.

Why?

Revenue agents would have difficulty filling out forms and calculating numbers if they splashed actual human blood on their hands.

That would leave the books soiled and perhaps illegible, hampering filing and calculating tasks.

Instead of physical violence, revenue agents wage psychological war against the human captives of the nation.

Revenue agents make threatening demands that humans pay sums, even sums clearly beyond their means, before absolute deadlines, or else they must pay more.

Complying or not complying will thus, at worst, render more humans suffering, homeless, and starving.

At best, the humans will be imprisoned with free room and board, until real criminals dispose of the revenue agent's prisoners.

23. DECLARING THE NATIONAL EMERGENCY:

The purpose of declaring the national emergency is to elicit and incite national loyalty and patriotism.

They are the essential life blood of the nation.

That blood carries the blind unconditional true patriot love and true believer zeal immortalizing the nation.

They make the nation invincible and invulnerable to all the reasonable, rational, well-reasoned, logical arguments and discussion about humanity's:

*common DNA;

*unifying physiological and psychological needs;

*mobile nature;

and,

*common human race solidarity, strength, and consequent advancement and evolution as a species.

Whenever an awareness of human commonality and a sense of human community arises and undermines or threatens the zealous and unquestioning devotion to the nation, the nation can depend upon the most reliable and effective remedy – the psychological panic force of declaring a national emergency.

The objective of declaring the national emergency is not to resolve an emergency, but rather to perpetuate it indefinitely so as to instill the feeling of insecurity and fear that makes national loyalty and patriotism seem essential to the humans who mistakenly believe that confinement within the national boundaries is natural.

The national emergency is intended to create such an exaggerated sense of personal insecurity that it miraculously transforms all the dreary routines, unfulfilling employment, occupational boredom or loathing, unequal pay for equal work, outrageously unequal distribution of wealth, unhappy lives, substandard housing, malnutrition, non-potable water, starvation, and all forms of discrimination into a status quo norm that is yearned for by all the people, no matter how badly off they mistakenly believe that they are within the national boundaries.

The national emergency confronts humans confined to the national boundaries with such a nagging and endless sense of great uncertainty that they are converted into desperate supporters of the nation and fanatical supporters of all its ills.

They expect nothing more from the nation than "a return to normal".

The national emergency is thus an extremely valuable tool for the nation and requires nothing beyond inciting fear of and anger with everything and everyone both outside and inside the nation.

The human self is threatening, but the nation is sheltering.

Unlike wartime, the nation does not summon the people to protect it.

Unlike wartime, the nation does not proclaim that their survival, way of life, and the nation itself depend on their help.

Instead, during the national emergency, the nation claims that its primary role is to protect the people.

It is an amazing reversal of diametrically opposite declared roles of people and nation.

It is a remarkable about face that goes unquestioned, unchallenged, and apparently unnoticed by the people.

The national emergency defines the outside world and all who venture, live, or visit there as threats to the people who are always confined to the nation.

The nation declares that those who go outside are the origin of all that is he bad, sickening, and killing, in short – every imaginable ill attacking the nation, such as:

crime, unemployment, terrorism, "world" pandemics, fuel shortages, pollution, environmental crises, etc.

These are all threats to the nation because they can cause all humanity to find common cause, uniting together in a struggle for all humanity instead of only the nation.

Fear of the "outside" hazards, threats, and mortal dangers enables the nation to increase its control of the people by keeping them and their minds isolated and quarantined from the rest of humanity.

Having created, fuelled, and maintained this mentality of fear, the nation can take the next step.

The nation can drum up support for punishing all the disloyal and unpatriotic people, i.e. the people who stray beyond the nation.

This also helps to drive a wedge between the unnational semantic concepts of civil and human rights.

The people are encouraged and persuaded to unwittingly differentiate and choose between civil and human rights.

If the nation is prime and life is only safe inside the nation, then only civil rights matter.

In the empty sockets of the eyeless nation, residents of the nation are nationals, not humans.

So they do not require human rights, which tend to endanger the nation and to be a contributing cause of the national emergency.

In reality, only nation rights matter.

The national emergency has the added benefit to the nation of increasing nationalism and inciting a new nation mentality.

When the national emergency is more severe in one province, prefecture, state, town, city, or other geopolitical locality than another, the less severely effected localities can sever contact with the others and form new nations.

The national emergency can thus lead to the births of new nations.

Every time that one locality blames another for problems that they have in common, to different degrees, the separatist spirit of new nation building can arise and flourish.

This further reduces the real, ongoing potential threat to the nation, i.e. that humans will realize that by working together as a united life form, humanity is far stronger and more successful as a species solving its pan-species problems.

The nation thrives on human disunity.

More nations means more divisions among humans, meaning a stronger nation entity and a weaker humanity.

When the nation is mortally threatened by human identity, unity, and mobility, it will declare the ultimate national emergency to destroy humanity with the nation's final solution – war.

24. MAKING WAR, TREATIES, TRADE, IMMIGRATION, AND CITIZENSHIP:

The main products of the nation are war, treaties, trade, immigration, and citizenship.

War is the greatest achievement of nation-making.

For war to be possible, the people have to be entirely persuaded that they should not consider themselves as only one part of all humanity.

The nation transforms other human beings into foreigners who can be attacked and killed as inferiors and as threats to the nation and its people.

Treaties are peaceful agreements to replace human relations with international relations.

The people accept complete exclusion from dialogue with the foreigners.

The nation can present treaties as compromises forced upon the foreigners.

Later, the same treaties can be condemned or declared broken promises of the foreigners.

Trade is an "exchange" of goods and services with the foreigners designed to make them look like dependants of the nation.

The foreigners should look even less competent than the people in providing for their own needs.

(Trade is described further in 25.)

Immigration and citizenship are meant to outlaw the natural historic migrations of human beings.

The people are told to consider themselves citizens.

The foreigners who wish to become citizens are told that they are immigrants.

(The foreigners' presence in the nation is proof that it is a superior place to live than everywhere else.)

No one can have a classification without the nation.

No one can move into the nation without the permission of the nation.

Through wars, treaties, trade, immigration, and citizenship, the nation demonstrates its effectiveness as an entity dedicated to eliminating the global identity, movement, and communication of human beings.

25. CONSTRUCTING THE NATIONAL WALL AND FREE TRADE AGREEMENT WITH TARIFFS:

Constructing the national wall and free trade agreement is a single act. One necessitates the other.

The nation must clearly demonstrate that the national free trade agreement does not mean the free passage of goods, services, and people both into and out of the nation.

Only national goods, services, and people will leave the nation, and only to serve the nation.

This means exporting, dumping, sending spies, and issuing temporary exit permits to people representing the nation's business interests.

No other goods, services, or people will be permitted to cross the national boundary.

The flow will only be one way, out of the nation.

Foreign goods, services, and people will not be permitted to enter the nation.

Besides, it would be cruel to raise the hopes of foreigners by leading them to believe that the national free trade agreement would ever actually allow their inferior products, services, and residents to enter the nation.

The nation's people are forewarned and offer no market for the foreigners.

The nation's people already know that all foreign things and persons are of no use or value to the nation, and are of very low quality.

Nevertheless, foreigners will predictably and desperately clamour to sign free trade agreements with the nation, knowing that without a free trade agreement with the nation they will be left out and doomed to never receive the superior goods, services, and people available only in the nation.

Foreigners instantly recognize that any-thing and anyone coming from the nation is a rare treasure of exceptional value.

While foreigners will quickly concede to every requirement commanded by the nation, including tariffs, to gain the unde-served honour of signing a free trade agreement with the nation, the national construction contractors will already be far advanced in planning an impenetrable wall to ensure that undesirables, i.e. foreign goods, services, and people will never successfully breach the national boundaries.

The national wall will extend beyond the official national boundaries.

Foreigners will happily pay this tribute of vast tracts of land to the nation, on top of tariffs, to demonstrate their overwhelming gratitude to the nation for permitting them the great privilege of signing the national free trade agreement.

The national wall will be built high, with the hardest available, impenetrable, reinforced, unbreakable materials, embedded with every type of intrusive electronic surveillance equipment imaginable, protected by many layers of barbed wire and legions of heavily armed guards.

Any foreign goods, services, or people attempting to enter the nation will be eliminated.

26. PLANNING NATIONAL TRAVEL:

National travel is planned to prevent the people from visiting the nation; to bolster their appreciation of the nation; to provide foreign aid to the handicapped and disadvantaged, (i.e. the foreign tourists); and, to create and reinforce negative impressions of foreigners.

The people will find it cheaper to travel outside the nation than within it.

Thus, the people will only experience the expense, inconvenience, and discomfort of travel while they are outside the nation.

The people will return to kiss the national ground, to repeat far and wide their stories of the horrors of travelling outside the nation, and to say, for the rest of their lives, "How lucky we are to live in the nation."

The people will thus understand why all foreigners want to travel to the nation and why they want to live in the nation forever.

This is why the nation must plan national travel with great vigilance, to discourage foreigners from travelling to the nation.

Foreign visitors can be discouraged by using a system of restricted visas, very intrusive security checks and demands, accompanied by numerous high fees.

Every foreigner will be fingerprinted and have his/her mug shot taken, as if s/he were a criminal suspect being booked and a convicted criminal being incarcerated.

Since foreigners are considered criminals by the nation anyway, because they are so different from the people, foreigners are no doubt already accustomed to such treatment and will know that they deserve it.

Of course only foreigners willing to give the nation and its tourist industry a huge amount of money should qualify for very limited access, i.e. short-term tourist visits.

Planning national travel thus helps to ensure that most foreigners can never set foot inside the nation.

This is the ultimate form of foreign aid.

Letting foreigners enter the nation freely and easily would be cruel because they are doomed to return to their dreary, disadvantaged, mediocre existence outside the nation.

Foreigners who somehow do succeed in coming to the nation for a visit should arrive wondering why they are bothering to go through all the inconvenience and humiliation in the first place, and why they are spending such large sums of money for their visit.

The reason, they should conclude, is that the nation is far superior to all other places and thus more than worth the effort.

The process of gaining the rare and wonderful privilege of being admitted for national travel should be so arduous and distasteful for the foreigners that they will arrive with unpleasant or hostile feelings about the nation.

Thus, the people of the nation will immediately recognize the unhappy facial expressions of the foreigners, and conclude they look that way only because they do not live in the nation.

Foreigners will also be instantly recognized as undesirable malcontents who can never truly appreciate the wonders of the nation.

As a result, these questions should be paramount in the minds of the people of the nation who encounter foreign visitors:

Why do foreigners have no manners?

Why are foreigners so rude and disagreeable?

Why don't foreigners stay home?

Why don't foreigners go back to where they came from?

Successfully planning national travel thus helps the people to almost instinctively know that all foreign places and visitors are troublesome, annoying, and not worth knowing.

This, by extension, is also the ideal model for planning national immigration policies and for greeting newcomers to the nation.

27. BUILDING THE EMPIRE:

Building the empire simply means redrawing the national boundaries to enclose more area.

War or treaties can be used to expand the boundaries, depending on the foreigners' acceptance of the nation's rule.

The empire is created to draw the attention of the people away from the problems of the nation; to turn foreign areas into places which really are worse than the nation; and to make the people fanatics of the nation.

28. ACTIVATING THE NATIONAL ARMED FORCES AND POLICE:

The national armed forces and police are bureaucrats wearing uniforms.

The armed forces are bureaucrats displaying rank on their uniforms and hats.

These bureaucrats have an arsenal of weapons of mass destruction instead of an assortment of office equipment.

These bureaucrats will attack, capture, maim, and kill people when ordered to do so by the nation.

The police are bureaucrats with badges and short range lethal weapons of less destruction.

These bureaucrats can threaten, detain, interrogate, jail, charge, assault, and kill anyone, anywhere in the nation, at any time, if they believe that such action is appropriate within the nation.

Unlike bureaucrats without uniforms, the national armed forces and police have no need for the pretence of acknowledging the participation of the people in the nation.

Bureaucrats in uniform are activated when subtle, nonviolent pretence and persuasion are not effective enough for the nation.

The people's role in the nation is unchanged.

Within the military, as within the nation as a whole, the objective is to instill a devotion among the ranks to obeying the nation without thinking.

Force is required because some of the people need to be neutralized, in various ways, while others need to be persuaded that not supporting the nation can be a frightening and potentially fatal experience.

In addition, compulsory military service is created so that the people will, at a young age, memorize prose, songs, and marches proclaiming the glory of being a member of the nation.

Compulsory military service will condition people, at a young age, to follow the orders of the nation without question.

Military training is the nation's obedience school for the people.

Anyone failing the obedience test can be posted to danger spots, where s/he is most likely to be incapacitated or eliminated by "accidents", "friendly" fire, or "enemy" attack.

No matter what happens, the difference between the nation and the military becomes insignificant.

Final words
(for the national library and archives)

By some error or lack of attention on the part of the nation, this volume of Terrian Journals invades the files of a nation's library and archives holdings.

The nation would normally censor, ban, and burn this volume and the entire Terrian Journals series.

The volume and series survive in the stacks only due to a lack of readership and, more importantly, the fact that this writing is the creation and publication of someone living within the boundaries of the nation.

The nation commands that all the written and otherwise recorded works of national creative minds be sent to the national archives and library, yet without imposing national censorship.

The purpose of the national archives and library is to store and preserve only the works and publications of the people of the nation.

This virtually compulsory deposit excludes all works created and published outside of the nation-state, whether authored by foreigners or not.

This is because all works created and published outside of the nation are contaminated by the undesirable impact of foreign influences.

These works are thus doomed to be mediocre, inferior, and not worth knowing about or storing and preserving.

For human beings deprived of all stimuli for creativity and stripped of all curiosity by the confinement, isolation, and immobility demanded by the nation, the presence of writings such as <u>Terrian Journals' How To Make The Nation</u> in the national archives and library makes that institution perhaps the sole positive aspect of the existence of the nation-state.

Access to knowledge beyond the nation can get people thinking.

VOLUMES FROM MYTHBREAKER
Terrian Journals series:
A Sketch of Terrian History
Terrian Journals' How To Make The Nation
Terrian Journals' 500 Years In Louis Bourbon's Few Hectares
Full Employment: Not Fulfilling
Terrian
Caretaker Society
Terrian Journals: Living as a Newcomer
Middle Earth Journals
Re discovery Journals
Fukurokuju No Kasumi Journals

Sabbatical Journals
Departure Journals
Adventuredate Unknown Journals
Away Team Journals
Searching For South Journals
Inonakanokawazu Journals
КАЗАНЬ Journals
Exile Journals
Tenjin Journals
Next Journals
Homeland Return Journals
Terrian Journals for the Misguided
Terrian Journals' N.S.R.: Not Spying, …Really!
TJ JNG: Terrian Journals' Jokes Nobody Gets
Terrian Journals' Half Serious
Terrian Journals' Iwitfulness
Terrian Journals' A Funny Bone To Pick
Terrian Journals' Disbelief
Terrian Journals' House Trap
Terrian Journals' Virtually Camping
Terrian Journals' Crystal
Virtually Dead
Terrian Journals' Maximum Insecurity
Terrian Journals' Mandarinas
It's News To Me
Terrian Journals First Anthology
Terrian Journals Second Anthology

Pre-Terrian Journals:
Explorations Of Inner & Outer Space
Out of Context
Terrian Journals Origins

Archway series:
Archway: Six Year Book of Dreams
Archway: Lifetime Rhyme
Archway: Life Before Dreams
Archway's Valentine Love
Archway's Garden Rhymes
Archway's Christmas New Years Rhymes

Additional Titles:
Language Learning Secrets
Trying To Teach Languages In The L.B.E. World
An Adult Book About Education
Terrian Journals' Miss Schooling?

Fiction: Terrian Journals' Political Science Fiction

www.ingramcontent.com/pod-product-compliance
Lightning Source LLC
Chambersburg PA
CBHW070808280326
41934CB00012B/3105